MARINE
CARVING
HANDBOOK

MARINE CARVING HANDBOOK

The design and making
of billetheads, trailboards,
and other marine carvings.

by Jay S. Hanna

International Marine Publishing Company
Camden, Maine

Copyright © 1975
by International Marine Publishing Company
International Standard Book Number: 0-87742-052-1
Library of Congress Catalog Card Number: 74-33147
Printed by Maine Coast Printers, Rockland, Maine

To the Other Urchin
who taught me the difference between A, B, and C
and much else besides.

Contents

IN GENERAL 1

WOODS 4

FIRST TOOLS AND A FIRST PROJECT 6

STERN BOARDS 18

BANNER OR RIBBON ENDS 27

DOLPHINS 34

ROPED EDGES 40

BILLETHEADS 44

TRAILBOARDS 55

STERN EAGLES AND OTHER BIRDS 60

OTHER USES OF DECORATIVE CARVINGS 74

FINISHES 76

TOOLS 80

SHARPENING 87

WHAT TO LOOK FOR AND WHERE 91

IT AIN'T EASY 92

MARINE
CARVING
HANDBOOK

IN GENERAL

Some of the joys and frustrations that come to anyone running a one-man shop and doing the same work for money that others sometimes do for a hobby are the continual letters and visits from people seeking advice, and my shop has been no exception. It cuts into the working time for which I can bill, and thus reduces my income, but I must admit to the double pleasure of meeting some very nice people and being flattered to have my opinion sought. Many times, the questions asked have no definitive answer without a demonstration followed by practice on the learner's part, and my shop isn't set up for teaching. Besides, I dislike other people using my tools: they get used to the way I handle them and don't take kindly to anyone else giving them directions.

So this book is for all you good people who want to try carving decorations in a traditional marine design for your boat or house. There's nothing here about wood sculpture, soap carving, or linoleum-block cutting, just marine carving. Enjoy yourself.

Someone once wrote that the art of ship's carving is dead. Don't you believe it. It may be old and is surely tottering around with a cane, but it is kept alive by small injections of enthusiasm and skill from professionals and amateurs alike. It would be hard to find a Rush, Skillen, or McIntire today — three of the many highly skilled men who carved life-size figures to grace the bows of seventeenth century ships — but there's always someone around to do what little carving is needed. That might be someone who earns part of his living at it, like me, or someone who wants the satisfaction of doing it himself, like you. No one, let alone me, can put down words that will make you a master carver, but this book can help you get started on the right heading, and perhaps it will keep you away from some of the shoals.

Ship's carving is an old and honored art. The addition of decorative carvings to vessels reached a peak of absurdity in the 1600s and 1700s. Why were the ships of that time loaded down with so much nonfunctional art? Partly because of pride in the vessel and to "show the flag" with great grandeur, but partly also for the same reason that Detroit puts chrome and racing stripes on a new car: to sell the product. Naval architects and yard owners had to sell a new design to an admiralty board, most of whose members didn't know the pointy end of a ship from the other end. If the model were covered with carvings, they could understand some of what they were buying and were more likely to appropriate the money for the whole.

By the time of the clipper ships in the 1850s, hull designs had been cleaned up and simplified, and the great head structure and its bracing were gone — and with it, the quarter galleries and multidecked sterns. Without all this structure

2

to decorate, and with an eye to the dollar (remember, these were merchant vessels, not Navy ships; they had to earn their way), designers reduced the carvings to a simple few: a life-size figure with a carved scroll to rest on in the bow, and perhaps an eagle on the transom. Pride of ownership kept this much decoration; besides, it was good advertising.

Shipbuilding and ship design constitute a traditional art, and even though our own vessels are pretty small today and most can only be classed as boats, we do like to carry on tradition and have some carving on them. What lady isn't more attractive with a little decoration?

There are no descriptions of how to carve a life-size figurehead in this book; few of us could use one on our boats, and, besides, I've never done one. We will concentrate on what can be used — billetheads, trailboards, quarter boards, and stern decorations. If you have the money and no interest or desire to butcher a piece of nice wood, there are carvers who will design and execute what you need. Look well and critically at their past work, because carvers, like any other breed, come with good, poor, and in-between abilities. Decide on the one who does the type of work you enjoy. But I do hope that you'll try carving your own. It's a pleasure to carve if you've been sitting in an office all day making those important decisions that keep the company, or the country, running. You may cut a finger or take a chip out where you want it in, but a little cussing, some glue, or a band-aid usually keeps things rolling. Carving helps to fill in those long winter evenings that "they" always talk about, and it keeps your thoughts of summer cruising active. Besides, in the spring you can do a little chest expanding to your admiring fellow boatmen.

For your use, I have included design drawings with squared spacing for enlargement, but I hope you'll also venture to create your own designs because the real enjoyment comes from seeing your own ideas in three dimensions.

Most courses in manual skills have the student making "practice" cuts, lines, or what have you, before completing anything that could be called a finished product. Now I haven't anything against this system for the other fellow, but I get bored making a whole series of practice anythings. I've been told that I wanted to be a Michelangelo first time out, but the truth is, I think most of us would prefer to have something to show for our labors. Then, too, assuming you are perhaps willing to scrap your first efforts if the final results are poor, it's better practice to work on an actual piece, the design of which demands more discipline in your cuts.

WOODS

The woods you use for carving are like boat designs — they are all a compromise. I'll give some of the pros and cons, and you pick what
4

you want to work with, the only real limitations being availability and cost.

The general rule is simply the softer the wood (barring balsa, which is useless in carving), the easier it is on your muscles. Balancing this, the harder and more close-grained the wood, the sharper and crisper you can carve details and the better the carving will resist abuse and aging. Straight-grained wood is, of course, the best. It's hard enough at first to get the tools to do what you want them to do without fighting twisty grains and knots.

Clear white pine is ideal to start with. It cuts easily, and it's so soft you'll have to watch yourself to keep from cutting off too much. It's good to use a wood that you have to be careful with, as this trains your hands to move the tool only where you want it to cut.

Mahogany is a little harder to carve, but for a rich look to that finished nameboard it certainly beats painted pine. If you can find it, get Honduran mahogany because of its even, straight grain. But look at a piece of Philippine mahogany and you'll see belts about half an inch wide in the grain pattern. You'll find that the grain goes up in one belt and down in the next, making carving with the grain a game of musical chairs. It can be carved, of course, but unless you have a good vocabulary of cuss words, don't use it as a beginning wood.

And so we come to teak, the best wood to use around the water. If you need much of it, fill your pockets with gold before going to the lumberyard. In spite of the fact that teak will take the edge off a circular-saw blade, it isn't all that hard to carve. You'll have to sharpen your tools more frequently because the abrasive in teak has a great dulling ability, but the wood carves beautifully. It is, however, quite brittle and it's very easy for a short-grained piece to break off. But with care, sharp tools, and, of course, that skill you're going to acquire, you can handle it.

Oak is a wood long used by English carvers, but it has streaks of soft and hard grain that make it difficult for the less-than-expert craftsman. Apple and most of the fruitwoods are lovely to carve and look at but are difficult to find.

Most big suppliers of boat lumber have short ends and blocks that are ideal for carving projects.

FIRST TOOLS AND A FIRST PROJECT

Carving tools come in dozens of shapes and sizes and, if you have enough money, you can easily go out and buy sets that will be the envy of us all. With this abundance of riches you will find that most of the tools will be like money in cold storage, seldom used but there when needed. Really, very few tools are needed to start with, and you can add to them as your interest increases.

Don't be conned into buying sets of small,

6

short-handled "carving tools." These are great for linoleum-block cutting, but not for the kind of carving we're going to do. What you need are tools long enough to get both hands on for control, and these are usually known as "professional" carving tools.

Instead of listing pages of tools at this point and scaring everybody with their variants and cost, I'll just go ahead and carve something and show you what you need for that job. If we start with a traditional bow or quarter nameboard that you can use on your boat or house, you can do the whole thing with three or four tools that won't put you in debt to some friendly loan office.

The first of these is a knife. Yes, a knife, and it can be used for more than crudely carving a heart and initials on the old apple tree. Not, however, a jacknife with a folding blade. It's prone to fold with your finger between the blade and the handle, and the resulting bloodstains spoil the work. A sloyd (an all-purpose knife with a short, fine, fixed blade) will do for most uses. With this tool alone you can carve a quarter board. To make the work go more quickly, you can add a half-inch chisel or a V gouge (parting tool), and a hand fret saw if you don't own a scroll saw or band saw. You don't *need* these tools, but they will lessen the effort expended.

No work that you do will be better than your layout, particularly the lettering. Why people will spend hours carving something with

loving care, but not spend the initial time making a good design, I'll never know. Maybe they are too anxious to get started, but it's a long way back when the finished piece is spoiled by a poor appearance. A misspelled word can easily be corrected on the drawing, but I've never been able to get an eraser to work on a carved letter. Poor looking nameboards are usually at fault in the size and spacing of the letters, so take your time before you go digging holes in a good piece of wood. All letters are not the same width or the same distance apart. The spaces between the letters are as important as the letters themselves. The distance between two straight-sided letters such as N and M should be greater than between two O's. O's, S's, and other curved top or bottom letters should extend above and/or below the line very slightly. Borrow a good book on lettering from your library for more information.

If you don't feel up to designing your own letters, most stationery stores have sheets of letter templates of various sizes. Trace the ones

8

Fig. 1. Letters slanting forward at the bow (above); vertical on the quarterboards at the stern (opposite page).

you need and cut up the paper into separate letters. Arrange these on a sheet of cardboard, and back and fill with them until the spacing looks good — nothing cramped and no wide-open gaps. View the lettering from across the room. Squinting your eyes also helps you see the balance between letters and white spaces. Remember, most viewing of the board will be from a distance. For this reason lettering should be in a simple style and somewhat bold so that it will be legible. (If you are operating a rum-runner or other illegal craft, use Old English or German Gothic, which is almost impossible to figure out). When you're happy with the arrangement, cover the layout with tracing paper and make a complete drawing.

Lettering on the old sailing ships was sometimes slanted to fit the lines of the vessel (Fig. 1);

Fig. 2. A nameboard with a simple feather end with a land for a screw. This is a quarterboard's traditional proportions.

lettering on the bow would slant forward, paralleling the stem rabbet line, whereas quarterboards would have vertical lettering. Because the space they were made to fit was narrow, most letters were stretched out. If you want to be traditional, follow these proportions. Nothing looks worse than a nameboard that's shaped like the cover of a shoe box.

Nameboard end designs can be as simple or as elaborate as you wish. A simple "feather" end with a land for a screw is shown in Fig. 2, but use your own imagination if you wish.

Get your hands on a nice clear, dry piece of white pine at your local pattern or cabinet shop — about 5/8" thick for a small board, 3/4" thick for anything longer than two feet. Have them plane it to thickness and cut it to the width you want. Transfer your art work with carbon paper — use a sharp pencil — and be sure to go over all the lines.

If you are going to finish your board bright, it might help to stain the surface before laying out the letters. This way, every cut that meets the surface has a definite line between light and dark wood.

10

Two things pertain to all your carving work: lighting and wood grain. Carving at a bench with the light directly overhead will flatten out the cuts. Have the light coming in from the side, so that shadows will show all unevenness. What looks good under an overhead light can be embarrassing when seen on edge in the sunlight. I'll talk about wood grain shortly.

A word here about sharpness. The most useless tool in the world is a dull one. So if you don't know how to get an edge that you can shave your arm with, read the section on sharpening now.

Clamp the piece down to your workbench — protecting the work face with a pad between it and the clamp jaw — and pick up that knife. In this exercise we will incise the letters with a V cut at least 1/4" deep. The deeper the cut, the bolder the shadow line in the finished letter. Don't be weak-kneed about depth in any carving; it's what you want. With the knife, make a cut down the center and ends of every letter (Fig. 3A). This is known as a "stop cut," and it is just that: it stops the wood from splitting away. Now, if all you own is the knife, make a sloped cut with it to remove the wood from each side of the line (Fig. 3B). Don't try to take it all out at once. Leave at least 1/32" near the outside edge for final cleanup. You will have to repeatedly cut down the centerline as you go. The ends of the letters may be cut vertically or on the same slope as the sides (Fig. 3C). This is the

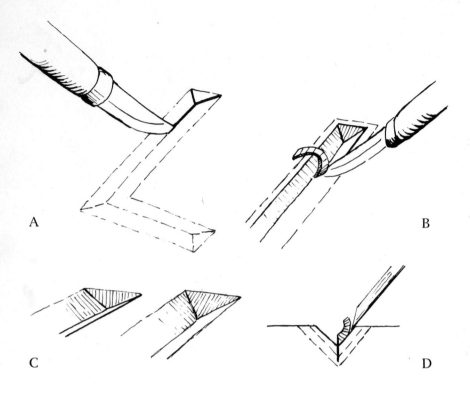

A

B

C

D

Fig. 3. Cutting in V letters on a nameboard.

old "heart on the apple tree" carving, but nice work has been done this way.

If you are using a chisel as well as a knife, make a series of cuts into the centerline — after making stop cuts with your knife — leaving clean-up wood at the edge as before. Make the final cuts with a paring motion along the length of the line. Cut only as much thickness at a time as you can control (Fig. 3D).

If you are right-handed, push the tool with your right hand, cupping the handle end in your

12

Fig. 4. Two methods of holding the carving tool.

right palm. This hand also does most of the steering. The fingers of your left hand hold the tool near its cutting end, and perform the duplicate operation of fine steering and holding back the tool to prevent it from overcutting. If you have some unaccustomed muscle ache at the end of the day, that's what did it — pushing with one hand while holding back with the other. There really are no hard and fast rules for where your hands grip the tool, so find the position that is the most comfortable for you. (See Fig. 4.) Final cleanup cuts are done more with fingertip control than with your full hand.

A carving tool really doesn't care if you are right- or left-handed. In fact, carving a curved line or surface is like beating upwind: it can't be done all on one tack. Mounting the work on a corner of the bench will permit more movement of your body in relation to the board, but you will still find times when it's necessary to

13

shift the tool to the other hand, so learn to use both hands. It's not all that difficult.

Except for roughing out, all carving should be done as much as possible with long, easy cuts so that the finished job looks carved, not picked at. If you are using a V gouge, the carving should be a series of progressively deeper cuts. Be careful to stop in time at the end of each stroke.

Because most people have heard it so often, it hardly seems worthwhile to talk again about wood grain, and yet it is forgotten at times in the enjoyment of carving. You can't always cut with the grain; probably about half your work will be across it. Try to make sure that the grain runs *into* the area to be cut, not out; then if a split starts, it will be into wood to be removed. Of course, this is not always possible to do. If you are using a V gouge and the grain runs slantwise to the cut, one lip will be cutting with the grain, and one against it. The answer here is fine cuts and sharp tools, and once the initial cut is made, remove material with the edge that is cutting with the grain.

Remember — many small cuts, not a hacking out of large splinters!

Assuming now that your lettering is carved, all that is left are the decorative ends. Fig. 5 shows a simplified traditional "feather." The squares on the original are 1/4" divisions, but they can be enlarged to any size, depending on the width you want. The first step is to drill a body hole for the size of roundhead screw that

14

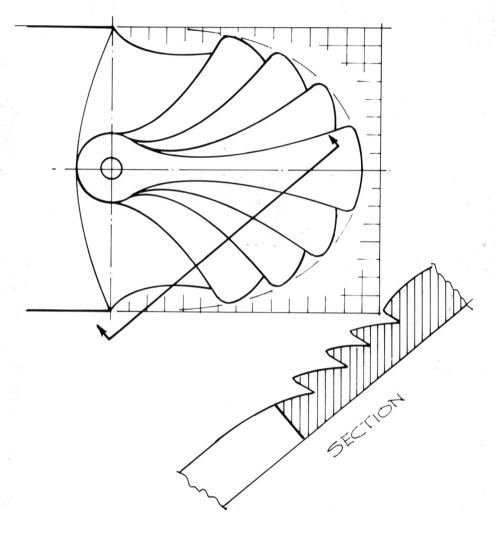

SECTION

Fig. 5. A design for a simple feather at the ends of a
nameboard.

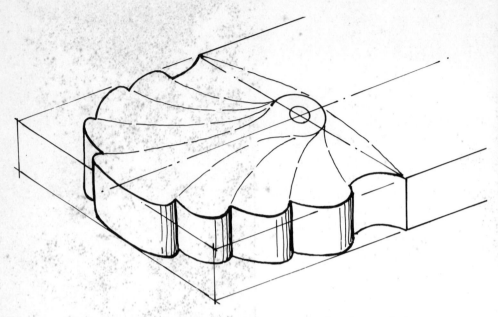

Fig. 6. A three-dimensional view of a feather and the stock it is cut from. First step in the cutting of the board ends.

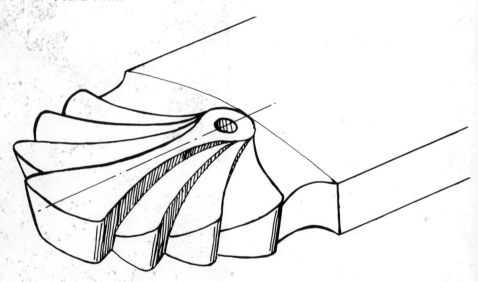

Fig. 7. The lines of the feather stand out better when the edges are beveled toward the back. Second step.

Fig. 8. A slightly more elaborate feather end.

you plan to use for attachment (Fig. 6). Next cut the outside shape with either the knife or a fret saw, scroll saw, or band saw. Now make the stop cuts along each line, and then pare the bevels with the knife or chisel. If you used the chisel on the letters, you held it flat, face down, to get a straight line cut. On these curving surfaces, turn it over, bevel side down, to get a sweeping curve. Leave enough of a land around the screw hole to support the screw head. To make the lines of the feather stand out more, bevel the edges in toward the back, as shown in Fig. 7.

If the board is to be finished bright and you haven't already stained it, do so now. Carry through whatever finishing schedule you are us-

17

ing, right to the last coat of varnish, then go back to the letters and ends to seal and paint them. This way, if you overrun the letter outlines when painting them, you can wipe off the surface with a cloth just barely dampened with turps or paint thinner. A good looking board can be had by painting it black all over, with letters and ends yellow or gold-leafed. Don't paint carved letters black. As I've said before, the shadow lines are what brings out the carving, and shadows show up very poorly on black.

Now that the board is done, look at it very critically to see what you would do differently next time. The things that will be the most obvious to you are where the chisel slipped, or where you didn't cut a curve just right. Put the board away for a couple of months (the paint really has to harden, doesn't it?), and then bring it out. By this time, you will have forgotten those places where you made the little goofs, and you'll see the board as others see it. Looks pretty good, doesn't it? So you say, "If I can do that, I can carve a stern eagle." So you can, but how about another cut or two along the practice route before trying?

STERN BOARDS

If you're ready to take a chance with a bigger piece of wood, let's consider a transom nameboard. Again, design is the big thing. Do a lot of

18

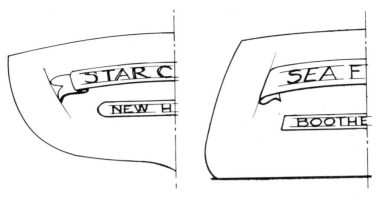

Fig. 9. *The curves of a nameboard should fit in with the shape of the transom.*

doodling and sketching. The primary controls are, of course, the shape and size of the transom, and the goal is a nameboard that fits. You don't want a billboard, but neither do you want something that looks too small.

Large powerboat transoms seem to carry much larger lettering in proportion to their size than do sailboat sterns. Now you can say that this is due to the larger ego of the powerboat owners, or to the shy retiring nature of sailboat owners; or maybe it's because the powerboats go by so fast that you have to be able to read the name quickly. Of course, a large stern board is a benefit to the sailor who wants to know who he's swearing at when a passing powerboat wake nearly swamps him in a narrow thoroughfare. Conversely, it gives him a chance to mentally thank by name the true powerboat sailor who slows down for him.

The curves should be agreeable with the transom shape (Fig. 9). If there is a lot of rake

19

to the transom, a board viewed from astern will be foreshortened in height. Letters on a curving board will appear somewhat less curved. You have a chance to let your imagination run wild on designs, but work toward the conservative end of the scale. Remember that it's a boat, not a circus wagon, that you're embellishing. One board for the name and another for the port of call is a good arrangement. This helps if you goof; then only part of the work goes in the stove. You can carve ornaments — stars, dolphins, or other traditional motifs, or something original to fit the name. Our boat's name, *Urchin*, came about because she was sort of raggedy when we got her; the sea urchins on her stern board relate the name to the ocean (Fig. 10).

A gentle or graceful name should appear on that kind of a board; likewise a strong name should be reflected in strong design and lettering.

Remember that you are working in wood, so don't make fragile units or intricate carvings that will break off. No water-holding hollows in the carving, either — everything should slope so that drainage is easy.

At this time you should give some thought to how the board is to be fastened to the transom. The first thing that comes to mind is through-planking screws, with the heads inside the transom. However, this can pose problems in a wooden boat with a decked-over stern: one, it may be difficult to locate the screws so that they hit neither seams nor frames; two, it may

20

Fig. 10.   Decorations on nameboards work best when they relate to the name of the boat.

be hard getting to the inside of the transom to turn the screw. On a fiberglass boat it might not be so difficult. The greatest objection I have to this is putting through-holes in any planking. A boat as old as ours has enough leaks without our drilling holes in her — even if they are above the waterline.

Screws put in from the face of the board are easier to get at, and need not penetrate through the transom. Flatheads can be sunk and plugged, which looks well, but they are difficult to remove. Roundheads that show can sometimes be worked into the design, as we will do on the sample nameboard; this method is by far the easiest and most practical.

The board can be drawn up tight to tne transom, and, if this is to be done, it's a good idea to put a good fat bead of flexible bedding compound on the inside edge of the board before installing it. Without the compound, there is a good chance of water getting in between and starting rot. I prefer to use rubber or neoprene washers (from a plumbing supply house) between the transom and the board. This permits drainage and ventilation and allows for minor discrepancies in fitting.

Most transoms have an athwartship curve that the nameboard must follow. If the curve is very slight, the board can be sprung to the transom with the fastenings. To aid a spring fit, make vertical saw cuts on the back of the board (about 1/2" apart and not quite half the board thickness in depth), across the middle three quarters of its length. If you follow this procedure, squeeze some flexible caulking into the saw kerfs before bending, to seal out moisture. On excessively curved transoms, the board will have to be bent to fit. The actual curve can be taken off by spiling.

One fairly easy way to spile off a curve is shown in Fig. 11. Draw a centerline down the transom. Then, find a light board somewhat longer than the proposed nameboard. Draw a centerline across it and nail equal-length spacers at each end, equidistant from the centerline. The spacers must project far enough to include the transom curve. Hold the board against the

22

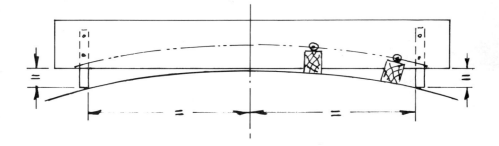

Fig. 11.   Spiling off the curve of a transom.

transom with the centerlines in line, and, with a
pencil held against a block that slides along the
face of the transom, draw a line on the board.
This will be easier if you nail the pencil to the
block with staples.   Back in the workshop, remove the end spacers and place another board
alongside the first.   By turning the pencil and
block around and following the first line, a
second line can be drawn on the new board.
This is the transom curve.

The bending should be done after rough-
sawing the shape of the board. You won't need
a steam box; just wrap the board in rags and pour
hot water over it. Keep it hot-wet for a while,
then clamp it to a form with the right curve and
leave it to dry. Of course, you can cheat and
avoid the whole bending bit if you design the
board with sloped end pads, as in Fig. 12, but,
frankly, the results aren't exactly appealing. A
board with end pads looks good on a flat surface, though.

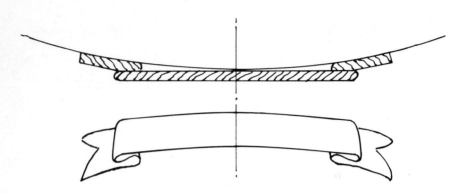

Fig. 12.   Using sloped end pads on a curved transom.

There are two types of carving, one of which we've already tried — carving in, which is termed *incised*. When the carved part stands out, it's a *relief* — bas-relief if it's low. (The "bas" in bas-relief is pronounced as a Mainer says Bar Harbor, or as a sheep says "baa.") High relief stands out more and so has more shape. It's also more prone to breakage and requires thicker wood to begin with — two of the reasons why we see more incised work on boats today.

Banners or wide ribbons seem to lend themselves best to nameboards and are simple and quite effective.   The middle is usually kept smooth, and the ends are waved, curled, or tapered. Most of the curling is an illusion fostered by the outline shape of the board and emphasized by enough surface carving to create shadows. Soft and gentle surface curves and slowly rounded edges lose their effectiveness because they don't have strong shadows. (See Fig. 13.)

24

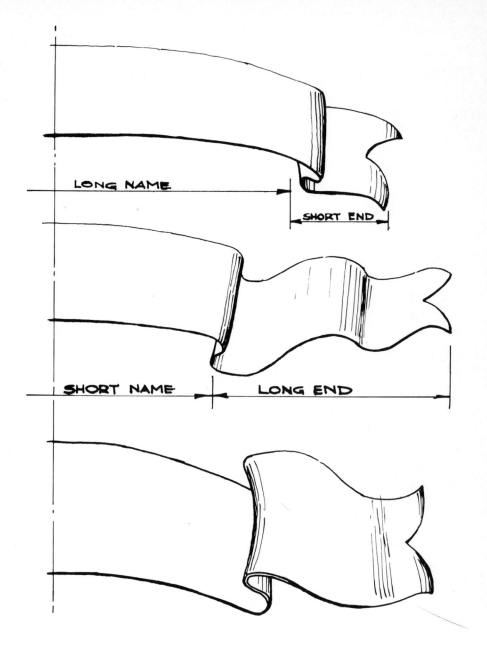

LONG NAME

SHORT END

SHORT NAME

LONG END

Fig. 13. Three banner designs.

Board ends can be finished off with the ever popular stylized dolphins or other fish. If you are doing something like the dolphin shown in Fig. 19, you can band-saw out the fish shapes and epoxy-glue them to the upper surface of the board ends. This gives you material for high-relief carving, whereas the letters are incised. By using just the board thickness alone, an effective job can be done in low relief. Cut a deep V outline at the intersection of the fish and board, and model the fish. Of course, if your boat is named *Pequod*, you'll want to change to whales and paint them white. Stars are more satisfactory if incised. Actually, a star in relief looks nicer, but the points where the grain crosses are very fragile.

A roped edge board is another old favorite. Again, this can be done in low relief the same height as the board surface, or it can be added on and then carved. The rope ends may be a Flemish coil, a fancy knot, or whatever your imagination dictates. Designed and carved nicely, rope makes a good looking border, but unless you don't mind repetitive work, you're going to wish by the time you're halfway through the job that you'd never started. But bear with it, you can't go sailing yet anyway.

What else can you do? Carve birds in the board ends if your boat has a bird name. Or carve one separately and mount it between the name and port of call. I don't know what you can do if you have one of those hybrid names

26

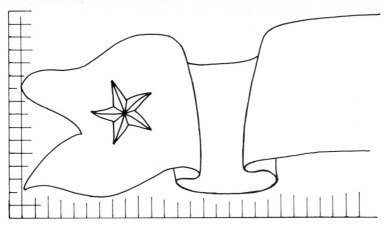

Fig. 14.   A banner end design.

made up of the first two letters of several person's names. You named her, you figure it out.

On this job I hope you'll do more carving and increase your tool range. If you're using a harder wood than pine, a mallet will save you much labor. A wood carver's mallet looks something like an old-fashioned potato masher. It has the advantage of always having its face in line with the tool end, and it is used with taps, not hammer blows.

BANNER OR RIBBON ENDS

Banners — or ribbons, as they are called in old English carving books — are reasonably easy to carve and look very well for the effort expended. But the carver must take the time to analyze the curves and surfaces involved. The wood cannot be thinned down to the thickness of an actual ribbon, but should appear as if it were.

Make a drawing of the banner end on tracing paper (Fig. 14), transfer it to both ends of

27

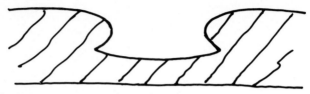

Fig. 15.   Cross-section of an undercut curl in a banner.

the work piece, and saw away the waste. I find that it helps to draw a line on the vertical edges to indicate roughly how the end is to be folded and waved, and to provide a guide for cutting depths.   Our example was carved from 3/4" pine and was thinned down to about 3/8" in the center of the return fold. With the board clamped to the workbench, "set in" (that is, outline and block out the shapes) and cut out the center groove.   Remember that the outline of the piece is what dictates the surface you are carving, except that you are foreshortening the curves in depth.   Use a sharp inside-ground gouge, and cut across the grain.   Make the top edge of this surface a little flatter than the lower, as the distance across the top appears to be greater.   In other words, think of this as a ribbon and curve it accordingly.   Round the edges of the top surfaces as they curl down, and undercut the curl slightly (Fig. 15).

The easiest way to carve the reverse curves at the bottom is first to cut across them, parallel with the lower edge, with a U gouge. Make one curve for the top curl and one for the bottom curl. Redraw the curl line and round the vertical outside curves. (See Fig. 16.)

28

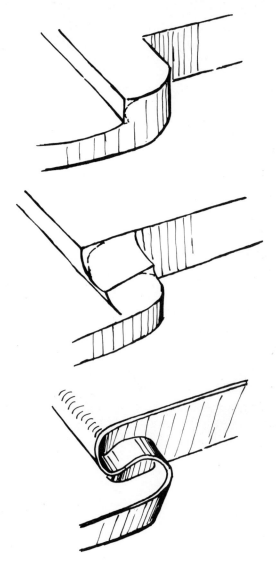

Fig. 16.   Carving the reverse curves at the bottom of a banner.

Fig. 17.   Carving a banner.

Now for the tricky part. Consider the bottom edge of the ribbon, inboard of the curl. It's a vertical surface (with the board clamped to the bench). Following it along outboard, carve it vertically until you come to where it rolls back. Carve the horizontal surface in to meet it. Repeat on the lower curl. It's harder to say than do. Undercut the verticals slightly, except for a narrow strip that indicates the ribbon thickness. Now put some waves in the ribbon end. Because the ribbon end divides into two separate pieces, you can carve the wave differently in each to give it more life.

The star is a simple, straight-line, incised carving. On a light piece of cardboard, draw a circle the size of the star's outside diameter. Divide the circumference into five equal parts and connect the points. Cut out the star, and you have a pattern that will conform to the waves in the board. After drawing around the pattern, draw lines connecting each point with the opposite indent. These are the lines, from the center out, on which to make your stop cuts. (See Fig. 18.)

To finish up, bevel back the top and bottom edges of the board, the top to a greater degree. Stand the board up and view it from slightly above, checking to see that it looks the way you wish it to. Painting the edges of the board black also helps produce the illusion of thinness.

32

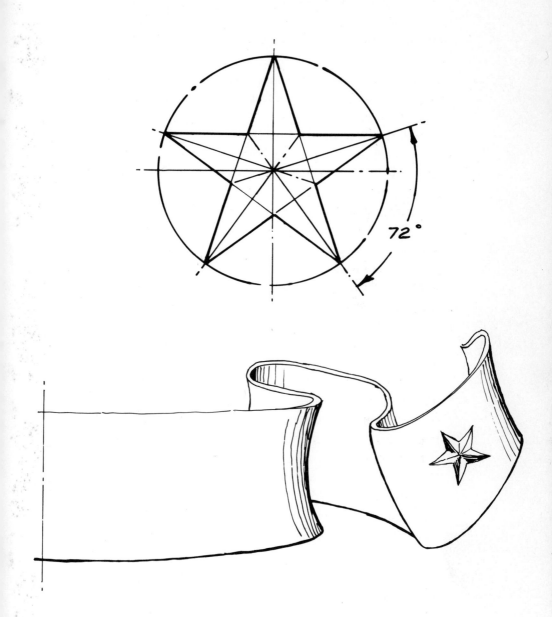

Fig. 18.   A star for the end of a banner.

DOLPHINS

Let's try carving a dolphin for a specific example, although almost everything said in this section applies equally well to carving a bird, a whale, or a horseshoe crab.

No one says that you have to use my dolphin drawing (Fig. 19); it's just to illustrate the techniques. First of all, in all the nautical miles I've covered, I've never seen a fish like this. However, as I stated, marine carving is usually traditional, and this drawing approaches the traditional dolphin design. Look up the drawings of fish that decorate old charts, or look at photos of old carvings; then draw your own if you wish, or use this one.

The simplest approach to the carving is just to cut grooves everywhere there is a line. For this you need a veiner gouge (a gouge that cuts a deep, narrow U). The effect of roundness in this case is achieved by the way the dolphin is drawn. Notice, for instance, that the scales are not drawn in a random pattern, but in a way that leads the eye to believe there is a roundness to the body.

If, instead, you make the outline cuts deeper, you can then emphasize the shape by low-relief carving.

After tracing the design on both ends of the board, making sure that one looks to port and one to starboard, saw out the waste. Setting in is next. I used a knife, a 1/4"-wide chisel, a

Fig. 19.   A dolphin design.

1/2" gouge (inside-ground), and a mallet. When cutting down around the design, don't try to cut the whole depth at once — take it in steps. Also, cut a little outside the lines so that you have something left for the finish cuts.   The lowest flat plane that forms the background for a relief carving, in this case the area between the head and body, is known as the "ground," and cutting and levelling it is part of the setting-in operation.   Grounds can be cut as smoothly as possible or tool marks from a nearly flat gouge may be left as long as they are not so

35

pronounced that they detract from the design. In this carving the ground was about 5/16" below the board face. Fig. 20 shows the work at this stage.

Make stop cuts around the hair, fins, and eye, then start lowering and rounding the shapes. At this stage, I added the use of 1/8" and 3/8" skews, 1/8" and 1/4" gouges, and a 1/8" bent skew. This is a good time to add some tools to your collection; the skews are handy tools for getting into corners. Unlike the carpenter's chisel or firmer, which is beveled on one side only, carver's firmers are ground equally on both sides. In addition, the skew firmer is ground at an angle to the tool axis; this way, it can get into corners. For tighter corners with high sides there are "bent" tools, which are bevelled on the top edge. A right and a left bent skew should be early additions to your tool drawer. (See the section on tools.)

With the whole design blocked in and rounded out, start with the highest details; in this case the hair, or mane. The swirls were cut with the 1/8" veiner, as was most of the detailing. Use the 1/4" gouge for wider and shallower valleys. The scales could be made as overlapping plates, but I made this carving in pine, in a rather small size (4 1/2" board width), so that method would have been pretty tricky. Instead, I just outlined all the scales with the 1/8" veiner to produce strong shadow lines; this way, I also avoided making fragile edges.

36

Fig. 20.   *A dolphin cut down to the ground.*

Fig. 21.   *A dolphin nameboard end.*

Rounding to the back of the board need be done at the top and ends only if this nameboard is to be mounted on a small boat, and hence viewed from above. And that's another thing about designing for carving: the viewing angle is important, particularly for surfaces that you wish to have appear thin or fragile. Fig. 22, which shows a profile view of a transom with sections at the top and bottom board edges, illustrates this.

Most "how to's" on carving tell you never to use sandpaper. I'll go along with this for some carvings, but not all. I just don't believe it should be regarded as a sacrilege. If you are an experienced Swiss carver who makes every cut clean, sure, and positive, then you don't need to smooth anything. Sandpapering a massive carving in oak can only detract from it. But for us unskilled workers in soft woods who are trying to make a decoration that we'll enjoy looking at, I think sandpaper can help in places. Just remember not to spoil what you have worked hard to get. Sharp, strong edges should not be rounded and lost, and tool marks that add to the design should not be sanded out. If you find that you can't round the eyeball of the dolphin smoothly with a tool, finish it off by filing or sanding. Sandpaper glued to flexible wood strips can be used as curved files, which you can conform to the shape you want. Emery boards (for fingernails) work well, as you can cut them to any width and shape you need in

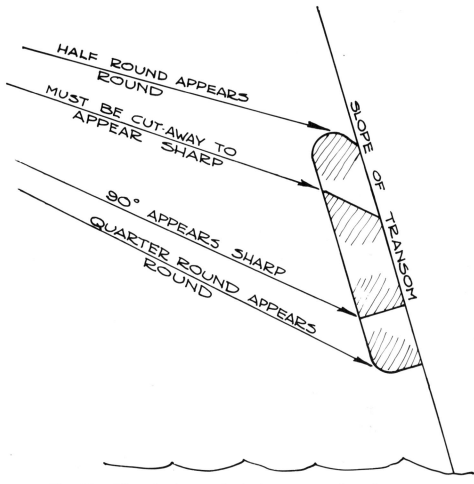

Fig. 22.   The viewing angle is important when designing the edges of a nameboard.

order to get into awkward places.   For finish work you can buy small files, both curved and straight, in many different shapes.   These are known as riffler files.   Do what you want to do;

39

but please don't hold a sheet of sandpaper in your hand and rub over the whole design.

When you are satisfied with your carving, give it a coat of primer if it is to be painted or gold-leafed. I like white-pigmented shellac for this job if the carving is to be used inside, as it dries quickly and stiffens the wood fibers. For outside work a good marine primer-sealer should be used. With the whole carving flat white, it's easy to spot places that need more cleanup. Look at the carving from all angles, and sharpen up any intersection of surfaces that are fuzzy.

So there you are with a nice looking board end. When doing a pair like this, it is smart to work on both ends, one step at a time, rather then completing one end and then the other. This way, there is more chance that the finished ends will look alike.

ROPED EDGES

A roped border is most effective if it is higher than the board it surrounds, but you can carve it using just the board thickness if you wish. In the latter case make a heavy V cut first, defining the edge of the rope where it meets the face of the board. The next step is to round the rope on the front and top edges and bevel towards the back of the board. (See Fig. 23).

To make a raised border, either cut down the face of the board inside the rope edge, a

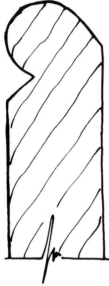
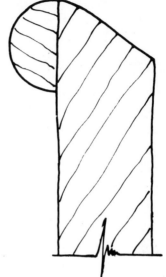

Fig. 23. A rope border that is not raised above the thickness of the board.

Fig. 24. A rope edge formed by gluing a strip of wood to the face of the board.

long job, or glue a strip on the face edge the width of the rope diameter and a little more than half the rope diameter in height. (See Fig. 24.) If you curve around the ends, it is smart to make that curve with separate pieces of wood to keep the grain running as nearly as possible with the rope axis. For assembly, use waterproof glue and small wire brads not driven in all the way. When the glue is hard, pull the nails; left in, they make carving difficult, and what they do to a cutting edge will keep you busy at the sharpening stone for quite a spell.

41

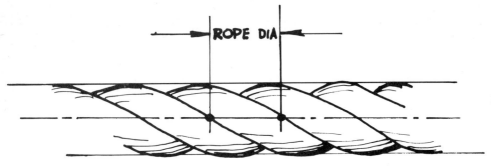

Fig. 25. Laying out the proportions of a rope border.

Let's assume that however you are making it, the rope border is now rounded and ready for the rest of the carving. To lay out the strands, run a centerline along the front face of the rope axis, and mark off spaces roughly equal to the rope diameter (Fig. 25). Cut a piece of light, flexible cardboard at an angle to its base of slightly greater than 30°. Roll this template over a dowel to give it a curve, and, with the base edge down in the groove, draw the strand separations. Now make stop cuts on each of these lines and cut in to a V, or use a V parting tool. Next, round each strand. Keep in mind that the strands are true rounds, and if it makes it easier for you, draw a centerline on each to indicate the highest part. That is, although we carved the overall rope shape with a horizontal axis, switch your mind around so that you think of each strand as a round with a diagonal axis. The need for this will become very apparent once you start carving the strands. If you keep a short piece of rope in front of you while

42

Fig. 26. The four steps in carving a rope edge (from right to left): marking, stop cuts, V's, and rounding.

working, there will be no problem. The intersection of the strands and the V cut of the board should appear as in Fig. 26, to emphasize the roundness of the strands. Fig. 26 shows the four steps: marking, stop cuts, V's, and rounding. Clean up the finished work with sandpaper sticks or riffler files.

For a roped border on the periphery of a transom, cut and fit together pieces of sized stock all around the transom, tacking them in place with fine-wire nails and keeping the grain running as nearly as possible with the rope axis. Number each piece so that they can be reassembled in the same order. Removed from the boat, they can now be carved in the shop. When carving at a joint, match the two pieces together to maintain continuity between the strands. This

43

can be done by lightly gluing the pieces to paper, which in turn is glued to a board. If the transom is curved, so must the backing board be, or the joints won't fit properly. After being carved, the rope can be split off the backing piece, and all the paper can be removed from the carving. Double-surfaced, pressure-sensitive tape works well instead of paper and glue, and is easier to remove.

If you are in doubt about achieving the right shape and curve to your backing board, just carve the strands except at the joints. Permanently assemble and fix the border to the transom, and then carve the joint areas. This method will result in the smoothest appearance — that is, unless you're attempting the job while the boat is afloat and you're in a dinghy. Rope work mounted this way should portray just half the rope diameter.

Rope carving is tedious; but done nicely, the finished job, all shiny with gold leaf, is handsome and well worth the effort. About halfway through you'll begin to wish you could just nail on some real rope, but stick with it. Real rope doesn't take on a good paint job anyway.

Good luck!

BILLETHEADS

One of the most effective bits of decoration on a boat is the one up forward that points the way, whether it's a figurehead dipping up and down with the swells, or just a simplified scroll called a billethead.

The first requirement for this type of decoration is a stemhead projecting out under the bowsprit. If your boat doesn't have a bowsprit, please don't finish off the bow with anything that looks like a head. It's fake and will spoil the appearance that a naval architect worked hard to achieve. A long, slim head should carry a light figure or billet. The point is to emphasize your boat's graceful lines, not to blunt or distort them.

Some billetheads are carved from the stemhead itself, but most are added on. The carving can be screwed or bolted on in the form of a rabbeted joint, which permits removal for repair or replacement in case of damage. It's also easier to carve a small piece that can be moved around on your workbench than to manhandle a whole stemhead.

On a boat with trailboards, the billethead design should be the forward termination of the trailboard design. The trailboard rails, top and bottom, run into and end in a swirl at the billet. Without trailboards, the billethead is just a nice way to end the stem; it certainly adds character and individuality to your craft.

Now that you are familiar enough with carving tools so that your palms don't get sweaty at the thought of cutting into that blank piece of wood, it's time to try something that you haven't

45

Fig. 27.   A design for a billethead.

tackled before: carving in the round. A billet-head really is two sides and an edge or face, but it will be a better carving if you think of the sides as part of the face. That is, roll some of the side carving around corners to make the design "in the round." The example shown in Fig. 27 has a minimum of this, but enough to introduce you to the thinking, so let's get on with it.

Because the billethead is to be carved on all sides, the holding problem is a little more complex than it was for a flat board. The easiest answer to this is to make up the block, and, having cut the rabbeted joint where the carving is to attach to the stem, make another block to fit the rabbet — sort of a dummy stem that can be held in the vise or clamped to the workbench (Fig. 28).

Fig. 28.   A dummy stem for holding the workpiece.

Fig. 29.   A billethead partially roughed out.

Having transferred the design to the block, on both sides, set in and cut down to the ground on the after end of the design. Next, drill holes for a couple of screws, one on each side in staggered positions, and fasten the two blocks together. Now band-saw the outside shape.

Notice in Fig. 27, side view, that the two round bands come in towards the center as they go forward, but that the center round that carries the star is the full thickness of the piece. Leave this thickness until all other carving is done (Fig. 29); it helps support the ends when the piece is clamped on its side on the bench.

Follow this progression in making the billet:

- Start with a piece of wood sized but twice the length of the billet.
- Trace the design on both sides.
- Cut the block in two on sloped aft line of billet.
- Cut the rabbet joint.

48

- Set in and cut down to ground at aft end of billet.
- Drill and screw to waste stock.
- Band-saw the shape.
- Set in around inner circle, and cut outer circle and bands to depth on both sides.
- Set in and cut leaves and stems to depth.
- Rough-shape leaves, stems, and outside rounds.
- Cut down center of face to depth, and finish shaping rounds.
- Draw centerline and curving "scales" on face.
- Carve scales.
- Finish carving all over.
- Set in edges of star.
- Cut down background around star.
- Make stop cuts on star.
- Slope down from center to points.
- Bevel point sides.
- Clean up all over.

I hesitate to tell anyone what textures to end up with on their carving; it's so often a matter of personal choice. What I did on this billet seemed to fit the design for me, but you do it the way you want to. I was going to finish off the outside rounds as a rope, but as the carving progressed it became apparent that in a small size this would appear too fussy, so I went to the other extreme and smoothed them round with sandpaper. I carved the next circle in with a shallow bent gouge, making the cuts from the

Fig. 30. *The various surfaces of a billethead (above, below, and opposite page).*

outside towards the center. This produced very subtle ridges and scallops, which I left, feeling that the tool marks were attractive. The face of the inner circle I dished in to the center; I carved the face smoothly so that the intersection of the star edges would be sharp.

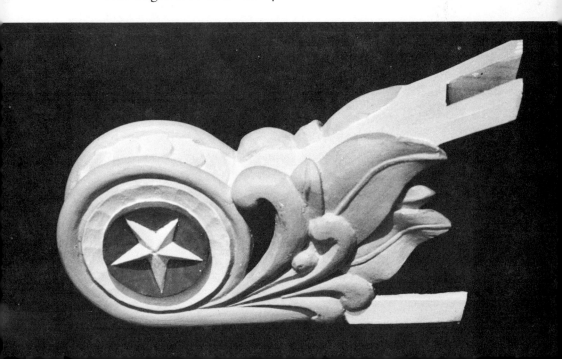

Again, I want to emphasize that carvings are personal things, and in most cases the drawing or pattern that you use should not be regarded as a must. What sometimes looks good on paper might not work in three dimensions. This is your work, and if you think the design can be improved while you're carving, go ahead and do it your way. Just temper your changes with the thought that, although you can easily cut more off, it's a little more difficult to put the wood back later if you don't like the change. In this same vein, if you break off a small chip on a leaf or other free-flowing design, it is frequently possible to recarve to a slightly different line to save the piece. This, of course, won't work on controlled motifs such as the star or letters. Use great care and take your time in situations where a slip would be costly. If you do slip badly, or if you find a pitch pocket or some other deformity in the wood right where you need a sharp edge (and this is, of course, where defects always show up), don't despair. You can drill out the bad spot and glue in a plug, or you can cut it out and set in a graving piece, which is just a rectangular or other-shaped block to fit your cut-out recess. Make sure that your added piece fits well, and that the grain and its direction follow the surrounding wood.

By this time, you should have a nice looking billethead for a decoration, a book end, or even for a boat that you can build to fasten to it.

52

Fig. 31.   A billethead mounted as a wall decoration.
(Photo by Graham S. Hanna)

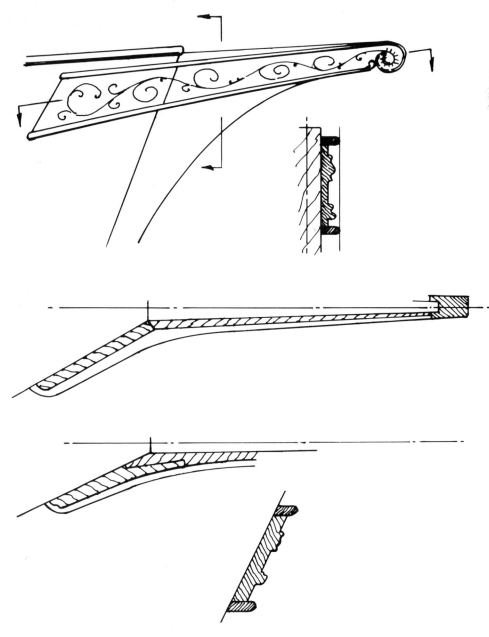

Fig. 32. Two different methods for making up a trailboard.

TRAILBOARDS

One wonders if the derivation of "trail" boards was simply "rail" boards, because that is the way they began. In the eighteenth century ships had numerous rails running aft from the stemhead as supports, and two of these rails remain today as trailboards. A trailboard, in effect, was made up of two long, slim knees, one above the other. These knees strengthened the stemhead in an athwartship direction, and vertically between them was the board that carried the decoration. The rails formed a curved knee where they met and ran along the hull. Some vessels had a definite break in the board at this point (the stem rabbet line), with one piece of wood on the stem and another on the hull; others had the board all in one piece or at least appearing so, with a curve instead of a break at the rabbet. This can be a tricky joinery job, but either way the design becomes complex. It's simple in the profile drawing, but boats are seldom viewed from just this angle.

Traditional types of boats, such as the Friendship sloop or the Chesapeake bugeye, have trailboard shapes and carvings that have become set for that type. If you are decorating such a boat, it is wise to follow in the tradition, at least as far as the shape goes. Friendships have a simplified vine decoration, but no one says that's the only thing that can be carved on them. Chesapeake Bay vessels have very long and slim trailboards that carry all kinds of designs. Besides a leaf scroll, the vessel's name is frequently worked in, and sometimes American shields or other motifs, so this type of boat offers great scope for your imagination.

Trailboards for a nontraditional type of boat can be designed to please the owner, but there are some rules to follow. The first is to keep all lines in harmony with the hull lines. The second is to remember that you are adding a decoration to the boat, not a billboard. I've seen some boards that completely destroy a bow shape, or that are gaudy enough to make a sea gull puke. The late L. Francis Herreshoff had the finest touch for good decorative design that I've ever seen, but why not? He believed hull design to be closer to sculpture than anything else.

Fore and aft lines follow and are directed by the lines of the bowsprit, sheer, and planking; vertical lines by the stem. The idea is to have a trailboard that continues the hull lines with no sudden breaks or dips. The upper and lower rails of the board are the defining lines, and these roll into the billethead and become part of it. All fore and aft lines should taper as they run forward. The total effect should be that the decorative work appears to be part of the boat, not something stuck on to dress her up. Remember, she's a lady.

I would suggest, if you are building the complete board, that you first make a pattern by taping heavy paper to the bow and stem, making

56

sure that it is pulled in to the rabbet, and then drawing the board and its rails. Remove the paper, carefully cut out the shape, and tape it back in place. This is a good way to observe how the board will look from different angles. If you are satisfied with the appearance, transfer the outside lines to the hull and stem. The next step is to make light pine patterns of the top and bottom rails with the correct bevels. For the rails to be kept horizontal in the athwartship plane, the part of the board lying on the hull will have to be made of pretty thick stuff so that it can be molded to fit the hull shape; and as I stated earlier, the board as well as the rails should be thickest at their after ends, tapering as they run forward. No one can tell you step by step how to construct the whole thing, but with these hints for guides, and good wood-working skills, you can do it.

The rails and board should be fastened together, and the unit should be held to the boat with screws. This way, when all is fitted, the complete unit can be removed for carving on the workbench.

What are you going to carve for a design? That's up to you. Usually, a major stem or branch runs the length of the board, with some type of floral scroll working off it: Ivy leaves for the Friendship; oak leaves and acorns signifying strength; or just an attractive convoluted pattern.

Incised carving is easier than relief. But if

57

Fig. 33.   Outlining a trailboard design in relief with V cuts.

you want it in relief, the easiest way is to outline the design with V cuts and round the internal
parts (Fig. 33).   For true relief on a small board,
you must recess all the background.   This, of
course, means that you must start with adequate
thickness so that the final piece will not be too
thin.   The total height of the carving should not
project beyond the rails or there will be no way
to protect pieces from being knocked off by
lines, boat hooks, and so forth.

*Fig. 34 (Opposite page). Carving a trailboard design
in relief.   The design has been cut out of a separate
board and glued and nailed to the background.
(Photo of the author by Paul A. Darling).*

58

On large boards, to avoid cutting away the great amount of background necessary, you can roughly band-saw the design out of another board. When I've done this, I've broken up the design into segments, for two reasons. One, you can get the grain to run more consistently with the design, and, two, it takes far less wood. With the design traced on the background, glue and nail the pieces to it. Use waterproof glue and finish nails. Don't sink the nails as you'll want to pull them out for the carving operation. After carving, they can be replaced and sunk for added strength.

On large work you can carve the face of the rails with a channel, cove, or beading, if you wish.

When the boards are complete and fastened to the hull, fit the billethead decoration. Again, I would emphasize that lines from the trailboard flow into and terminate at the billethead. Avoid any appearance of a "stuck-on" billet.

Head carvings are a major item of a vessel's appearance, so spend time on the design. The final result is too important to permit skimpy initial considerations.

STERN EAGLES AND OTHER BIRDS

From the very early days of this country, before nationalism was a dirty word, the American eagle in realistic or stylized form has probably graced more transoms than any other ornament.

60

Fig. 35.   A duck used as a transom ornament.

If you want tradition, the eagle is it. You can arch a nameboard over him, with a port-of-call board below, or the eagle can carry a lettered banner in his beak or claws. Design your own or find a design in an old book, a government seal, or an advertisement. Whatever you do, you should carve all his lines strongly.

If you don't care to make this positive a statement (I heard that phrase on a news broadcast), carve a sea gull, a duck, or even a dove. After all, the latter is what Noah sent out from the ark to see if there was a landfall to be made anywhere. Almost any of the sea birds make good motifs.

61

Fig. 36. A curved eagle being carved by the author on a framework built to the shape of the vessel's canoe stern.

Whatever bird you decide to carve, avoid thin, cross-grained parts. Tuck a thin beak over some other part of the bird; use undercutting to make something appear thin; or if your design doesn't permit this, carve the whole thing in relief on an oval board. Study the design well before starting, and work out the carving in your mind.

Because the carving is on a transom, which is usually curved, the same mounting problems occur that we spoke about in the section on nameboards. No steam bending will solve the problem here, but it is possible that a mild hollowing of the board back will produce a good fit. If the transom has an excessive curve, you will either have to add wood at the ends or resort to a thicker piece.

We once had to carve a six-foot eagle for a sixty-five-foot yacht with a canoe stern. This was done by making a template of the bulwark area to be occupied by the bird. Light pine boards were scribed to fit the top and bottom lines of the bulwarks. These were then connected by verticals that fit the slight up-and-down curvature. The whole contraption was then removed from the boat and taken to the shop. There I built a rugged framework that fit the pattern (Fig. 36), so in effect I had a section of bulwark to fit the bird to, and at the same time a jig for carving. This same procedure can be followed no matter what size your carving will be. It insures a good match to the hull.

If the back of the bird is to be flat, there's

Fig. 37. An eagle roughed out to establish the levels.

no problem. Hold the work on the bench with a carver's screw or padded clamps. If you haven't acquired a bench screw, read in the section on tools about making one. I use clamps to hold the work during all of the heavy roughing out, and I then use one bench screw in the center of the bird. This permits me to rotate the work, making carving easier, and to vary the angle of lighting.

If you have completed the previous, simpler carvings in this book, there is no need to repeat an explanation on handling your tools. You will, of course, block out the carving to rough shape, establishing the levels, that is, the thickness at different places on the bird, that you want (Fig. 37). After that, you can carve as simply or in as much detail as you wish.

I like to finish the eye first because its appearance is critical and because it puts life in the bird. If you spoil it or don't like its looks, the eye can be recarved without doing over the whole head. With the completed eye to keep watch on what you're doing, it's easier to keep the rest of your carving alive. And, of course, it's someone to talk to as you carve: a benevolent eye approving your praise when the chips peel off as they should, and a glittering, fierce one to receive your muttered curses when a feather splits. Forgive the old carver his strange ways, but things like this do happen when you work alone.

As feathers make up most of the surface, you should consider how you want to show them. They overlap much as fish scales do, from top to bottom; so after roughing in the surfaces, you should cut in the various rows of feathers — working from the top down — so as to produce an effect of curving clapboards (Fig. 38). When you have done this, redraw the individual feathers and shape them with their overlaps or steps. Actually, not even this need be done; you can just carve the sweeping, hollowed curve of the wing surface and outline a feather pattern with a veiner. A stylized eagle is treated in this way. John Bellamy, one of the great carvers of the late 1800s, made some stylized eagle plaques that are models of simplicity. Only a few, oversized feathers are outlined on the wings. All of the grace and beauty of the bird is expressed by the overall form, not by details.

65

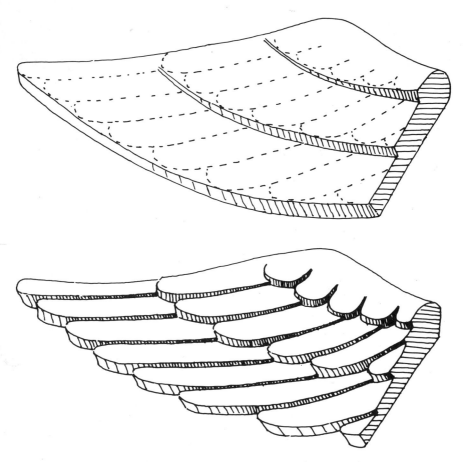

Fig. 38.   Carving the wing feathers.

Unless the complete design is simplified, I would carve the rows of feathers as I described in the paragraph above.   But again, there is a choice.   A simple and very effective treatment is shown in Fig. 39.   The center spine of each

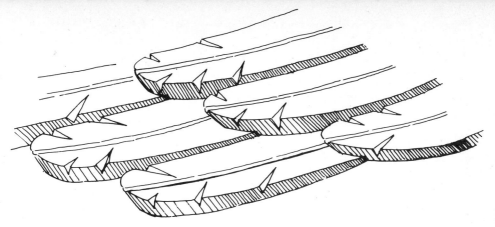

Fig. 39.   A simple treatment of feathers.

feather is simply a narrow V or U groove, and
random notches are cut into the feather edges to
indicate breaks in the barbs.

However, I have also seen examples of eagle
carvings in which each feather was elaborately
detailed.   The surfaces were waved at the edges
and looked soft.   Even if you don't wish to go
this far, you can carve the spine to appear raised
(which it really is) and put in some fine V cuts
to show the pattern of the barbs (Fig. 40).   Perhaps the best way is to try various methods on a
piece of scrap, and then decide which one you
want to use.   Don't count the feathers, though,
or you'll leave them all blank!

The beak and lower jaw are, of course, smooth
and are carved oversize with the back of these
parts distorted in depth to give them the necessary

Fig. 40.   A more elaborate treatment of feathers.

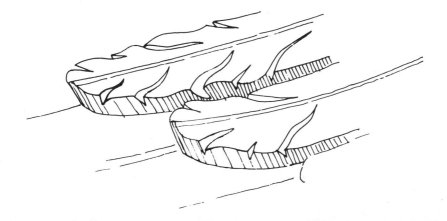

Fig. 41. A veiner can give the leading edges of the wings a downy look.

strength (Fig. 33). In our example I separated the ribbon into a front and back section where it went through the beak, but for boat use it would be stronger, if not as nice looking, if it were left solid. If the folds in the ribbon bother you, take a piece of cloth and pinch it as it would be held in the beak, and see how it looks. The way it folds on the ends shouldn't cause you trouble if you've carved nameboards as described earlier. Notice the way the ribbon slopes on the face surface (Fig. 42). Don't keep it parallel to the back of the board, but vary the surface. The head and surrounding area looks well if it is treated as hair with closely spaced grooves made with a veiner. The thighs may be done the same

68

way or covered with small feathers. In our example the leading-edge wing feathers were treated as was the head, a veiner being used to give more of a downy look (Fig. 41). They could instead be small feathers carved in the same style as the rest of the wing, or they could even be left smooth. The feet and legs are rather knobby with rings running around them. The claws or "toenails" are like the beak — very smooth.

You will have to turn the bird over once in a while to make the sloping-edge relief cuts. For this reason I left the four highest points (the wing "elbows" and the highest part of the ribbons) block thickness until almost the end, and used them as clamping points. Put an old piece of padded material, such as quilting, between the bench and the carving face to fully protect the face when working on the back.

Fig. 42. Two worm holes that require repairs on the ribbon face of an eagle.

The ribbon offers quite a bit of room for whatever lettering you wish. If the eagle is going on a transom, you may want to carve in the boat's name and port of call, or perhaps thirteen stars. For a pure decoration you could use Commander Lawrence's famous "Don't give up the ship;" or the 1812 slogan, "Fair trade and sailors' rights." These belligerent sayings go well with this eagle, as he is carrying only the arrows and not the olive branch as well.

Figs. 42 and 43 illustrate some repairs that were made in the wood. For this eagle I deliberately used an old piece of pine with a knot and some worm holes, so that I could describe repairs. Two of the worm holes appeared on the ribbon face. I ignored these until the roughing out was done, at which point I jammed two rough plugs into the holes for centers and then drilled them out with a 1/2" drill. I then made round plugs from some of the scrap sawed off during the initial shaping of the bird, making sure that the grain ran across the plug face. With the plugs and holes well coated with glue, I fitted in the plugs, the grain running in the same direction as the surrounding wood. The next day I cut the plugs off flush, and, when I completed the final shaping of the ribbon, they were hardly noticeable. In another area, where a worm had made a U-shaped gouge in the surface, I used a plastic wood filler, making sure beforehand that I had removed all loose dust from the worm's boring.

The knot disappeared in the carving process,

70

Fig. 43.   Plugs glued in the drilled-out worm holes. These plugs will be pared down flush.

Fig. 44.   A finished eagle.

leaving only some wild grain that necessitated careful carving in that area. So don't despair if you find poor areas in your carving block. Work around them if you can; if you can't, cut them out and replace the wood.

Once again, I'd like to comment on how you do these carvings. They should be expressions of yourself, so anything said in these pages is suggestion only. Follow the drawing in Fig. 45 if you wish, but if you argue with the way I do something, fine — do it your way. Design your own bird, think up a new way to do the feathers, and if you carve more than one eagle, make them different. If you like realism, visit the nearest museum that has mounted specimens and study them. If this doesn't appeal to you, go the other way. Simplify to the point where the bird's character is demonstrated by planes and outline. However you do it, carving is more than just a manual skill.

You can take other bird designs from illustrations in bird books and apply much the same carving techniques described here. A swimming duck or similar design need not have individual feathers portrayed; a better plan is to carve according to prominent color separations or whatever makes the bird distinctive. Look through books on carving duck decoys for tips.

Fig. 45 (opposite page). A design for an eagle.

72

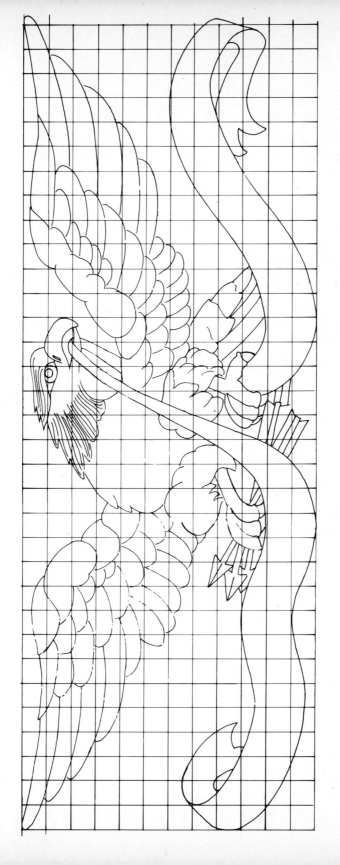

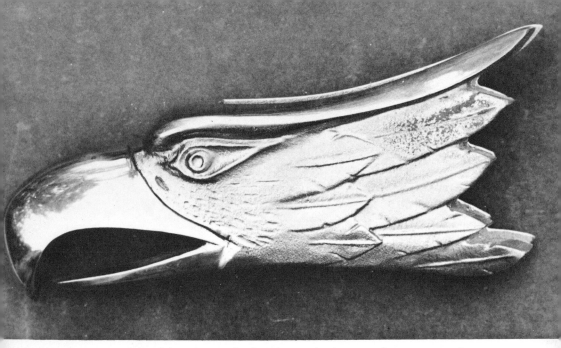

Fig. 46. An eagle head cast in bronze from a wood carving. (Photo by Graham S. Hanna).

OTHER USES OF DECORATIVE CARVINGS

Where else can you use carvings? Almost anywhere your heart desires. Some Dutch yachts use them everywhere, from the stem to the top of the rudderhead.

Tillers have long been a favorite subject for carving. The inboard end — where your hand rests — and the knob at the very end are frequently served, or wound with line in some manner, so as to form an antislip device and decoration. These effects can be made permanent by carving the tiller as though it were served. I once saw a French cutter that had this done, and the result was a real conversation piece, as well as being useful. The grip was

74

carved as cockscombing and was finished off at the ends with carved turk's heads. The knob carving simulated a monkey's fist, which is the knot used on a heaving line. A lot of careful work was required to make this tiller, but it was something I'd like to have on our boat. Maybe some day when there's time . . . If this interests you, obtain a copy of one of Hervey Garret Smith's books, such as *The Arts of the Sailor*. His drawings of decorative rope coverings look real, and they are a good guide for this type of carving. If you have the time, six-stranded coach whipping is ideal. The knob could be carved as a dolphin head, a human head, or any other round object that appeals to you.

In the days when sailing vessels had several levels of decks, the rails ended gracefully in scrolls or ogees (Fig. 47). If your boat has rail endings, this is another area where you can show your skills. The same type of carving can be done on the aft end of the cockpit coaming.

Some yachts today still carry catheads for the anchors, and these can be finished on the end with a cat's head, as were catheads on the nineteenth-century yachts. "Cat" in this case usually means a lion. The ever popular star is also a traditional ending.

Afloat or ashore, sea chests are attractive items of furniture, and bas-relief carvings of a nautical theme on their tops add a great deal to their appeal. The cupboard door panels in either the galley or the kitchen are other places for

Fig. 47.   Simple rail endings.

marine carving. An anchor, house flag, or other
simple design sketched with a veiner will do.
I can just see the enthusiast standing in the
middle of the kitchen floor, gouge in hand, a
wild look in his eye, thinking, "What can I do
next?" Enjoy yourself, but have a little restraint.

FINISHES

I have mentioned finishes previously, but a
little elaboration on the subject might help. We
already know that light and shadow emphasize
the efforts that you put into a carving. Say that
you had a house nameboard on which the letters

76

came out not quite as smoothly as you wanted. The board will be read quite close up — it's not meant to stop traffic — so contrast between letters and board is not of prime importance. Staining the board a medium brown and painting the letters buff or a dark tone will minimize the unevenness of carving. The flatter the paint, the more the carved surface will flatten. A semi-gloss paint will allow a few highlights, and a gloss paint even more, so you can subdue to any degree the apparent surface roughness. Working the other way, the lighter the color and the higher the gloss finish, the more every carved

Fig. 48.   *More elaborate rail endings.*

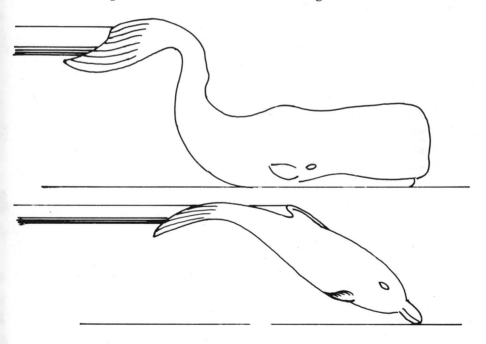

surface and line will show its shape. The ulti-
mate in richness is gold leaf.

Quarter boards and such look well when
finished bright with several thin coats of varnish
sanded between coats. Take care to brush out
any varnish puddles in the letters, and in sanding be careful not to round the sharp top edges
of the letters. After the varnish is dry and hard
(wait at least twenty-four hours after applying
the last coat), paint the letters, again watching
for puddles.

If your boat sports no brightwork whatever,
your feeling being that it is too gaudy, substitute
paint for the varnish. A black board with yellow
carving looks well as long as you subdue the
yellow a bit towards a buff color. Yellow is, of
course, the poor man's gold and has been used
extensively over the years.

The carvings on your transom or on your
billethead and trailboards can be emphasized
with some color if you wish, but don't overdo
it. Any national motifs such as shields, flags,
and stars can use red, white, and blue, of course.
Old-time figureheads were frequently painted in
colors, so the tradition is established, but please
remember that they were a small ornament on a
very large hull. Catch the observer's eye, but
don't blind it.

Gold leafing may be a time-consuming process, but once you've rowed out to your boat in
the morning and seen the water-reflected light
rippling across the carving, all the effort will be

78

worth it. Gold leaf is pure gold beaten out so thinly that pieces of it will float in the air. Don't use "gold" paint or powders: they are not true gold, and they turn brown after short exposure to weather. Leaf comes in little books and can be purchased as "loose" or "patent." Loose is exactly that — a sheet of gold between pages and free to be picked out. Patent gold for "gilding in the wind" is slightly adhered to a backing sheet and is much easier for the beginner to handle and use. See your local paint or art store or a sign painter to purchase gold leaf.

A good smooth surface is needed for gold leafing, and this is best provided by a marine enamel. The enamel can be almost any color, but yellow is preferred. Gold size, a slow-drying, varnish-type finish, is then brushed on smoothly and evenly. When the size has dried to the right tack, it should be tested with a knuckle. If it sticks to your knuckle, it's not dry enough; you should feel a slight pull and hear a light tick as you pull your knuckle away. Pick up a sheet of patent gold by the backing paper and lay it face down on the size. Rub the back of the paper evenly so that the gold adheres to the size. Continue this method, overlapping the sheets slightly. Any missed spots can be covered the same way. The next day, when the size is hard, burnish the surface (rub it gently) with absorbent cotton to polish and remove any excess gold. Do not varnish or otherwise try to finish over the gold, as this will kill its brilliance. Gold will outlast the rest of the finish, but be sure to seal and paint or varnish the back of the board as well as the front, so that no moisture can get in.

Applying loose-leaf gold requires skill, but is the fastest method for covering large areas. Preparation for gilding is the same as above, except that the handling of the gold sheet is different. The gilder uses a "tip," a soft brush the width of the gold sheet. The tip is gently brushed over the gilder's hair to mildly charge it with static electricity, and is then touched to one edge of the gold sheet. The gold can then be lifted and floated over to the work. Place the sheets so that they overlap slightly. Don't allow the tip to touch the size or become sticky in any way, or the gold won't let go. If you've been using fish oil to hold your hair in place, maybe you'd better stand under the shower before trying this method.

Gold leaf is also available in rolls of different widths for striping. This might be the most economical way for the beginner to gild letters.

TOOLS

If you have progressed to carving eagles and other reasonably large and complicated subjects and have found it interesting, then you will also have developed the wish to acquire more tools. At this stage of the game, the long list of available tools will not scare you out of the whole idea of

80

carving because your experience will guide you in determining what you need.

There are really only four types of carving tools — flat, U, V, or square-sided U — but by grinding or shaping them differently, the manufacturers come up with eight tools (Fig. 49).

Fig. 49.   Eight basic carving tool shapes.

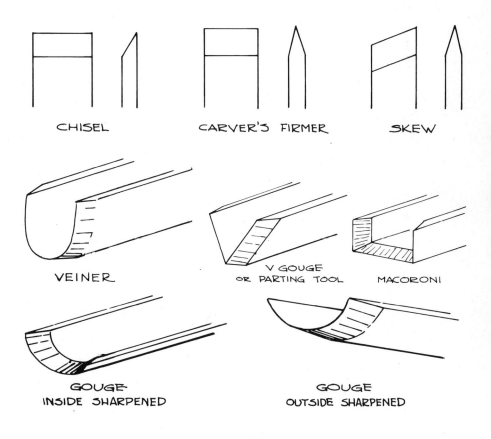

CHISEL   CARVER'S FIRMER   SKEW

VEINER   V GOUGE OR PARTING TOOL   MACORONI

GOUGE
INSIDE SHARPENED

GOUGE
OUTSIDE SHARPENED

There are five variants of these that make carving easier (Fig. 50). Each of these variants comes in about a dozen sizes, that is, if you can find a place that sells them all.

The gouges also come in varying degrees of curvature, or sweeps, from almost flat up to half round; and V's with cutting edges that form various included angles can be purchased.

Like most of us who enjoy working with our hands, I like tools. Even if I seldom use some of them, they are there to do a particular job when needed, and I delight in the way that a certain tool does that job. Besides, good tools have a functional beauty. Now if someone were to present me with a complete set of all shapes and sizes of carving tools, I'd feel as if I had the riches of the world; I'd make fancy drawers in a chest to keep them in. I also know from past experience that some of them would never be used. The truth is, you develop a liking for and a skill with certain tools, and you find ways to use them in preference to others. This is due partly to the feel of the handle and partly to the temper of the tool. All carving tools seem to vary in their ability to hold an edge. I have some gouges that stay sharp no matter how many knots I cut through, and others that in spite of retempering just can't cut with the smoothness I like.

You'll need various gouge sizes, but to buy them all would be foolish. You'd spend so much time picking up one and putting it down to pick

82

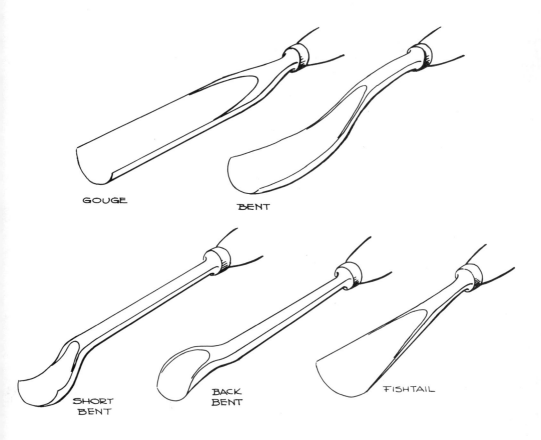

GOUGE   BENT

SHORT BENT   BACK BENT   FISHTAIL

Fig. 50.   Five variations of the basic carving tools.

up another that nothing would get done. It's quicker to take a second cut with the one in your hand.

So you're serious about carving and want a good all-around collection to work with? My choice would resemble the following:

Chisels and firmers — 5mm, 12mm, 25mm
Skew firmers — 5mm, 16mm

Skew short-bent chisels — 5mm, 12mm (one right-handed and one left-handed of each size)

Gouges (straight) — 5mm, 10mm, 25mm (one inside-sharpened and one outside-sharpened of each size — about a #9 sweep, a little less than half round)

Gouges (fishtail) 8mm, 14mm, (#5)

Gouges (veiner) — 1mm, 5mm, (#11)

Gouges (V parting) — 3mm, 10mm, (#12)

As you get used to these tools, you'll find that certain ones work well for you, and so you'll wish to acquire more sizes of that type.

Sometimes, unexpected tools work best. The daughter of a long deceased boatbuilder was cleaning out his shop and sold me a 2" slick and a 2 1/2" shallow gouge. A slick is a chisel blade of quite some size with a turned-up handle socket, this means that the bottom or flat of the blade can stay flat on a surface with the handle up out of the way. A slick should be fitted with a long handle, but mine had just a stump left. I was carving a great many half-models for builders at the time, and these two tools became my favorites. They had enough size and weight for excellent control, and they would take such a fine edge without breaking that I could use them as planes. It was a pleasure to see the paper-thin chips one could take off, using these tools.

So acquire your tools where you can. They certainly don't need to be a matched set. Once you have them, don't throw them in a drawer

84

to rattle together. As you've found out by this time, the best steel is no good if it's dull, and having loose tools bumping into one another is a quick way to dull and nick them. Some carvers keep their tools in a cloth case for protection, but I prefer shallow drawers with wooden holders or partitions to keep them separate.

Along with the carving tools are the added aids such as the mallet (Fig. 51), mentioned previously. You can buy beautiful lignum-vitae mallets, or if you have a lathe, you can make your own. Mine came from a small maple log out of the firewood stack, and a piece of locust that had been used to handle some tool a long time ago. You'll want enough weight in the mallet so that you don't have to pound with it. If you will be carving bas-relief panels that have large, recessed flat areas, a hand router (Fig. 52)

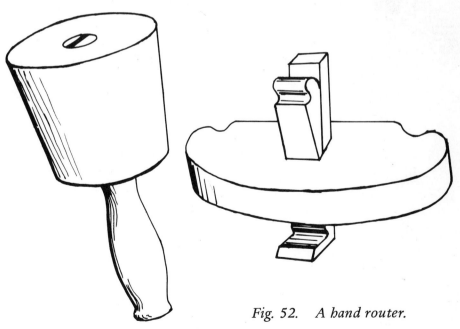

Fig. 52.   *A hand router.*

Fig. 51.   *A mallet.*

can be a benefit. Again, these may be purchased or made. For holding work to the bench, ordinary screen turn-buttons may be used, or bench holdfasts, C clamps, or, better yet, what the English call flat cramps, which don't stick up and get in your way (Fig. 53). Large work such as eagles can best be held by carver's screws through the bench top (Fig. 54). These can also be purchased or hand made. Mine are 1/4"-diameter lag screws, long enough to go through a loose hole in the bench top and penetrate the work about 3/4", with another 3/4" or so extending below the underside of the bench. Cut the head off the lag and thread the shank for a 1/4" wing nut. The end of the shank should have a screwdriver slot hack-sawed in it.

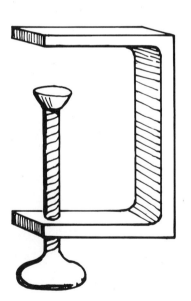
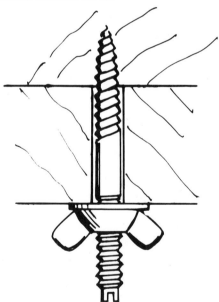

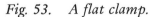

Fig. 53. A flat clamp.   *Fig. 54. A carver's screw.*

Years ago, my grandfather had a summer cottage in Maine. One fall, he failed to get a bill from the caretaker for the year's maintenance work. He wrote the old gentleman to inquire what he owed. (They were both State-of-Mainers and therefore very honest in their dealings with each other.) The answer came back, "I have lost the stick I stir up my desk with, can't find an account." This is all right for a desk — it's certainly the way mine looks — but please, keep your edged tools separated.

SHARPENING

Tools that are dull are worth no more than an old block with a split sheave. When someone confesses that he doesn't know how to sharpen tools and that he wants to learn, I'm full of sympathy. If he asks where to go to get them sharpened, I'm saddened; for there is no place close enough unless you have let out one corner of your shop to someone who can do it and is always there, and even that is like having someone to tie your shoelaces. The whole idea is something like writing with a sharp pencil: the lead may always be showing, but if you want a fine line, the pencil goes back to the sharpener every few minutes.

Most new tools come ground to the correct bevel, but only some of them are sharpened as well. There is a distinction here. When your tools need grinding, if this is beyond your capabilities, take them to a machine shop; for grinding is a once-in-a-while thing. Sharpening is putting a cutting edge on the bevel; it is a rather frequent thing and really not all that difficult. There are two methods of sharpening, and we'll discuss the old tried-and-true one first. A power grinding wheel develops so much heat in the tool that if the bevel were brought to a fine edge, the very thinness of the metal would permit overheating and the temper would be destroyed; to prevent this, we hand-rub the tool on a sharpening stone. Wanting to accomplish our purpose as fast as possible, we start with a coarse stone to bring the tool to a sharp edge, and then switch to a finer stone to smooth it. At the end of this operation there will be a "wire edge" that you can feel on the side opposite the bevel. The next step is to switch to a hard, very smooth stone, such as a hard Arkansas, and use it to polish the bevel edge. The wire edge on the side opposite the bevel will still be there, but one or two passes with the back of the tool flat on the stone will remove most of it. The edge is now stropped on an old-fashioned razor strop or an oil-soaked piece of leather tacked to the workbench. Stropping is passing alternate sides of the cutting edge over the leather to remove all traces of the wire edge. You should now be able to shave your arm with the tool. A trial cut on a piece of pine should leave an almost polished wood surface. Any whiter streaks or spots indicate duller areas on the edge. Go back to the hard Arkansas and strop again to remove these.

You can rub chisels over the stone back and forth, or with a rotary motion; take care to maintain the same bevel at all times. Gouges are more difficult: you must rock the tool from side to side as well as back and forth, so as to sharpen the whole bevel evenly. Be careful on the corners to keep the cutting edge a straight line; don't round them. Shaped "slips" are used to touch up the inside edges.

If all this sounds involved and you want to invest in power tools, there is a new sharpening system that is easier, quicker, and more accurate. This system is the Woodcraft Mark II and is available from the Woodcraft Supply Company in Woburn, Mass. It involves grinding with aluminum-oxide cloth belts in varying grades, and it produces little heat build-up, an advantage over the grinding wheel method. After grinding, the tool is honed on a buffing wheel charged with white rouge, which produces the final edge and polishes the tool. This system is expensive unless there is a great quantity of sharpening to be done, but it is an ideal setup.

If you have an electric motor that you can attach a buffing wheel to, it will eliminate the final honing and stropping steps from your hand-sharpening system. This is a great time saver, as these two steps should be repeated whenever tools begin to dull. Grinding and rough sharpening should only be done to remove nicks in

89

the cutting edge or to bring the bevel down after many sharpenings.

How do you tell that a tool is getting dull? By feel — is it getting harder to push? By the cut surface of the wood — is it no longer smooth and almost polished? By the wood fibers — are they tearing instead of being sheared off cleanly in end-grain cutting? Keep the edges honed and you will do a better job of carving.

WHAT TO LOOK FOR AND WHERE

For historical background and design ideas, see the following books at the library or bookstores:

The Arts of the Sailor, Hervey Garret Smith, Funk & Wagnalls, N.Y.

Marlinspike Sailor, Hervey Garret Smith, John De Graff, Tuckahoe, N.Y.

American Figureheads and their Carvers, Pauline Pinckney, Norton, N.Y.

Shipcarvers of North America, M. V. Brewington, Dover Pub., N.Y.

The Decorative Arts of the Mariner, Gervis Frere-Cook, ed., Little, Brown, Boston

For bird designs and colors these books are a great help:

Field Guide to the Birds, R. T. Peterson, Houghton Mifflin, Boston

The Ducks, Geese & Swans of North America, F. H. Kortright, Stackpole, N.Y.

Birds of America, T. G. Pearson, Doubleday, Garden City, N.Y.

Audubon Water Bird Guide, R. H. Pough, Doubleday, Garden City, N.Y.

Game Bird Carving, B. Burk, Winchester Press, N.Y.

For tools, try your local hardware and art supply stores, look in the yellow pages, or send fifty cents for a catalog to Woodcraft Supply Corp., 313 Montvale Ave., Woburn, Mass. 01801.

For wood, see your local shipyard, lumberyard, pattern shop, or furniture maker. If they don't have what you want, ask to see the catalogs of their suppliers.

IT AIN'T EASY

And now, assuming with complete faith that you have arrived at this point without becoming discouraged, I can tell you a story about an elderly Maine boatbuilder whose competence I admire. Years ago, I saw a piece of work that he had produced that involved some masterly carving. Really wanting to know his technique for achieving such results, I asked him how he'd done it. After scratching his head for a minute and looking puzzled, he answered, "Wa'al. . . it ain't easy." I'll never be as skillful as he is, but I'm beginning to understand what he meant. You can't say, "Do thus and so, and this is what you'll get." Carving isn't like bolting two metal parts together. The first time you "do thus and so" the results may be disappointing, but after letting your hands become familiar with the tools for some time, you realize you are turning out something quite good. Consciously, you are not aware of doing anything different from the first time, but somewhere along the way your hands have learned to translate to the wood what your imagination sees. So when your admiring friends ask, "How did you do it?" you too can answer, "It ain't easy."

92